RACE AND NATION IN THE UNITED STATES

RACE AND NATION IN THE UNITED STATES

A historical sketch of the intermingling of the peoples in the making of the American Nation

BY

E. A. BENIANS

Master of St John's College, Cambridge

A LECTURE DELIVERED TO STUDENTS OF BEDFORD COLLEGE
AT CAMBRIDGE I MARCH 1944

CAMBRIDGE

AT THE UNIVERSITY PRESS

1946

CAMBRIDGE
UNIVERSITY PRESS

University Printing House, Cambridge CB2 8BS, United Kingdom

Published in the United States of America by Cambridge University Press, New York

Cambridge University Press is part of the University of Cambridge.

It furthers the University's mission by disseminating knowledge in the pursuit of education, learning and research at the highest international levels of excellence.

www.cambridge.org
Information on this title: www.cambridge.org/9781107639102

© Cambridge University Press 1946

First published 1946
First paperback edition 2014

A catalogue record for this publication is available from the British Library

ISBN 978-1-107-63910-2 Paperback

PREFATORY NOTE

My object in the following lecture was to describe the intermingling of the peoples in the making of the American nation and the manner in which national unity has been attained. The lecture was delivered to students of Bedford College at Cambridge on 1 March 1944 and has been a little enlarged for publication. I am indebted to my friend Dr Dexter Perkins, at the present time Professor of American History and Institutions in the University of Cambridge, for reading through the manuscript and assisting me with valuable comments.

E. A. B.

RACE AND NATION IN THE UNITED STATES

☙

THERE are no peoples in the United States in the sense in which there are peoples in the British Empire or in the Union of Soviet Socialist Republics. The Americans are not one race divided into many peoples, but one people made up of many races. Or shall we say being made; for the American Republic is still young? We and our parents and grandparents have lived through the period when there passed through its open doors the great majority of the men and women who will be the ancestors of the American nation.

Under the old régime France colonised Louisiana as well as Quebec; but it is on the St Lawrence, and not the Mississippi, that there is a French people to-day. At the time of its conquest in 1664, the New Netherlands contained about 7000 Dutch inhabitants, while at the Cape of Good Hope in that year, there were not as many hundreds; but in South Africa, and not in New York, a Dutch people took root and flourished. The circumstances and policy of the British Empire have tended to pre-

(7)

serve nationality; the circumstances and policy of the United States to absorb it. Thus, while the British Empire resolves itself into a Commonwealth of Nations, the United States pursues the goal of national unity.

More remarkable still is the fact that Irish, Germans, Scandinavians, Poles, Italians, and indeed a dozen different races, have entered the country in numbers sufficient to form separate peoples, had they and the Americans so desired. Neither so desired. Thus, in the New World we do not see the diversity of Europe reproduced in a federation of peoples, but a new nation.

All Americans, except the Indians, are recent immigrants. The great majority crossed the ocean of their own will, to find freedom or betterment. They adventured because the New World seemed to them to offer better prospects than the Old. To them America was the land of hope. This prevailing motive governed their behaviour in their adopted country, their expectations and their reception. The national psychology early exhibited a confidence that the New World can offer something better than the Old. The relations of the different peoples with each other have been shaped by the task and the hope that they shared—to establish in a new nation a new order for mankind.

The nineteenth century was the great age of movement. Or, to be more exact, the century between 1820 and 1920. In those years more than thirty million people crossed the ocean from Europe to the United States. The development of steam transport made it physically easier and so cheaper to move than it had ever been before. The telegraph and the newspaper spread ever more widely a knowledge of the conditions and opportunities of America. Population was growing fast in Europe. Over-peopled lands saw far off a relatively empty continent. In Europe, at different times, in different places, in different degrees, were unemployment, poverty, famine, racial, political and religious discrimination and persecution: in America were employment, freedom, and opportunity. The inducement to move, the means to move, the willingness to receive, all coincided.

So the stream began to flow, fed from an ever-widening watershed—from the British Isles, from North and Western Europe, from South and Eastern Europe, and from the eastern shores of Asia, increasing the population of the United States by immense numbers of a great diversity of races. It swelled at times to a torrential invasion. It was the greatest migration of recorded history. At last the golden door was closed and the 'general invitation to the people of the world' withdrawn. The vacant lands were taken up, the field of employment ceased to be unlimited, the continent had passed beyond the initial stage of its development.

Such was the coming of the peoples whose assimilation and amalgamation are to form the American nation. As they distributed themselves over the continental space and became absorbed in the activities of American life, the country seemed a graveyard of European nationality.

When Jefferson addressed a famous declaration to 'a candid world', he wrote of 'our British brethren' and of 'the ties of our common kindred'. In 1776 this was no doubt true. Careful enquiries into the national origins of the American people have shown that the colonial population, excepting the negro, was substantially of British stock. Yet already many other races were represented. The first census, taken in 1790, did not distinguish native-born and foreign-born; nor was this done until the census of 1850, of so little importance seemed the question of the intermixture of races. Later calculation based upon it distributes the colonial population according to country of origin as follows: Great Britain and Northern Ireland 77%, Germany 7·4, Irish Free State 4·4, Netherlands 3·3; of the other nationalities represented, French, Canadians, and Belgians were the most important.[1] The total population in 1790 was about four million, of whom the negroes numbered three-quarters of a million.

In the seventeenth century the immigrants had been mainly English, but Swedes and Dutch had planted commercial settlements on the Atlantic seaboard. In 1680 a stream of persecuted sects began to flow from Germany, and, a little later, other Germans emigrated from regions devastated by war. The Scotch-Irish who came from Ulster—for British policy in Ireland pressed hard on Protestant as well as Catholic—were the largest group of immigrants in the eighteenth century, perhaps 200,000 in all, and, with the Germans, made up as large a number as the English immigrants of the preceding century. Scotland, too, was contributing. Boswell, travelling with Johnson in the Western Highlands in 1773, found a 'rage for emigration'. In Skye, a dance called 'America' had been introduced, apparently to show 'how emigration catches, till a whole neighbourhood is set afloat'.[2]

These eighteenth-century immigrants went

[1] Davie, M. R., *World Immigration*, p. 44.
[2] Boswell, *Johnson* (ed. Croker 1831), II, p. 502.

largely to the frontier districts, particularly of Pennsylvania and New York, where the fusion of races began. So the western halves of the colonies, from Massachusetts to North Carolina, tended to show some difference of race and character from the tide-water. The religious exclusiveness of the New Englanders kept them from mixing freely with the new-comers far into the nineteenth century. But elsewhere there was intermixture, especially in the middle colonies. To South Carolina had come West Indian planters and Huguenot merchants; Georgia had received Oglethorpe's immigrants. South of Pennsylvania the plantation system rested on slavery, and here were most of the negroes. In Georgia there were Indians. But, in general, the Indians retired before the white man and there was little intermixture. Disraeli wished that the republic of the Puritans had blended with the tribes of the wilderness. Raleigh, and, later, Colonel Byrd of Virginia (1674–1744), advocated intermarriage with the Indians. But this was uncommon in the East. It was the *coureurs des bois* on the St Lawrence and the Mississippi who brought in the Indian blood. A writer of 1810 remarks that 'only a few Americans have ever seen a native redskin'.[1]

[1] Brown, R. H., *Mirror of America*, p. 26.

The diversity of the population had resulted from circumstances. It was neither promoted nor prevented on theory. The colonists needed labour, and welcomed the kind of immigration that supplied it, whether British, European or African. They were not more, perhaps less, hospitable than their descendants. In small communities dissidents are more trouble than in large. The religious persecutions of Europe, however, taught the duty and showed the advantage of hospitality, and the English colonies became places of reception, though they showed different degrees of liberality in their treatment of aliens. At the Philadelphia Convention (1787) James Wilson, a Scot of Pennsylvania, mentioned that, when in Maryland, he had found certain disabilities there a continual vexation; he would feel it absurd to frame a constitution under which he himself could not hold office.

Thus colonial experience contributed to the making of the American nation. It produced a civilisation substantially British. The institutions and habit of self-government and religious freedom were planted in favourable and stimulating surroundings. The American too learned to welcome the immigrant. The intermixture of races began, and in the slave population the chief race problem of the future appeared. But we must remember that the colonies had not in mind an American nation. Great Britain could not persuade them to unite for defence against Indians or France. Local feeling was very strong, distances were great and means of communication lacking, and the manner of life was different in New England, the Middle Colonies and the South. As yet, the concept of America did not exist among these separated, diverse and mutually suspicious communities. But the conditions were favourable for national development and events brought it about. In the quarrel with England the idea of American unity and an American nation was born. At the Stamp Act Congress of 1765 a delegate said: 'There ought to be no New Englander, no New Yorker, known on this continent, but all of us Americans.' Then followed, step by step, the making of the Union— the Continental Congress (1774) brought the leading minds together, the Declaration of Independence (1776) set a goal, the Continental Army associated men in action and danger, the Articles of Confederation (1781) started them on the road to political union, the Federal Convention at Philadelphia (1787) produced the Constitution of the United States. So the political mould of the American nation was formed.

At the Philadelphia Convention the question of

the foreign immigrant was discussed.[1] The discussion revealed different points of view. It was clear that the proposed federal government must be empowered to establish a uniform rule of naturalisation; for citizens of one state of the Union must automatically become citizens of other states. But fear was expressed concerning a too free admission of foreigners. The fear was of their political opinions. Foreigners, said Gouverneur Morris, cannot learn our laws and understand our constitution under fourteen years; it will require time to eradicate native attachment and the affections of education. We should not be polite at the expense of prudence. As to those philosophical gentlemen, those citizens of the world, as they called themselves, he did not wish to see any of them in our public councils. Men who can shake off their attachments to their own country can never love any other. Nor could the legislatures be trusted never to choose improper persons— there was no knowing what legislatures would do. Others, however, stressed the economic advantage of admitting immigrants and the American tradition of liberality. Madison believed that great numbers of respectable Europeans, men who loved liberty,

[1] *Documents illustrative of the formation of the Union of the American States*, selected, arranged and indexed by C. C. Tansill, see pp. 505–6, 512, 524, 876.

would be ready to transfer their fortunes thither. He did not want anything illiberal in the constitution. America was indebted to immigration for her settlement and prosperity. Those parts which had encouraged it most had advanced most rapidly in population, education and the arts. Mr Wilson, of Pennsylvania, cited his own state in proof of this, and pointed out that three of its deputies at the Convention were not natives of America. The travelled Franklin sought to reassure the assembly. The people in Europe, he said, are friendly to this country. He would not discourage the common people in Europe from emigrating to America. The Convention saw the future as they saw the past; they could not foresee the multitude of emigrants. So the liberal view prevailed. The door was opened and Congress was left to regulate the matter.[1]

But, following the French Revolution, Gouverneur Morris had the satisfaction of seeing his prophetic fears realised. A good many philosophical gentlemen came and many good American citizens were alarmed. The Federalist party legislated to protect the rights of mankind from their French champions. A Naturalisation Act of 1798

[1] Viz. empowered 'to establish an uniform rule of naturalisation'. *Constitution of United States.*

extended the period of residence required for citizenship from five to fourteen years, and an Aliens Act empowered the President to expel foreigners. But these enactments awoke protests from Virginia and Kentucky, which laid the foundation of the doctrine of state rights and were to resound for long in American history.

While the politicians were discussing the admission of the foreigner into the American state, the people on the frontier had settled his admission into the American nation. In the old colonies, with fixed habits, prejudices and character, a new nation was less easy to visualise than in the backwoods, where life was forming afresh and civilisation had to be built up from its foundations. Here human qualities and capacities counted for more than differences of race. The welcome to the immigrant came from the frontier, where the battle with nature reached into the forest. 'In America', writes the Marquis de Chastellux in 1782, 'a man is never alone, never an isolated being. The neighbours, for they are everywhere to be found, make it a point of hospitality to aid the new farmer';[1] and St John de Crèvecœur, in his *Letters from an American Farmer* (1782), pictures the forming of the

[1] Marquis de Chastellux, *Travels in North America in 1780, 1781 and 1782*, quoted in *The Heritage of America*, edited by Commager, H. S. and Nevins, Allan, p. 255.

new type, the American man, as the incoming peoples mingled in the West. 'Here', he writes, 'individuals of all nations are melted into a new race of men, whose labours and posterity will one day cause great changes in the world.... The Americans were once scattered all over Europe; here they are incorporated into one of the finest systems of population which has ever appeared and which will hereafter become distinct...'. 'What then is the American, this new man? He is either a European, or the descendant of a European, hence that strange mixture of blood, which you will find in no other country. I could point out to you a family whose grandfather was an English-man, whose wife was Dutch, whose son married a Frenchwoman, and whose present four sons have now four wives of different nations. *He* is an American, who leaving behind him all his ancient prejudices and manners, receives new ones from the new mode of life he has embraced, the new government he obeys, and the new rank he holds. He becomes an American by being received in the broad lap of our great *Alma Mater*.'[1]

Thus was set forth the principle on which the American nation was to be formed—'race inter-

[1] *Letters from an American Farmer* with preface by W. P. Trent (1908), pp. 54–5.

mixture on the basis of political and religious equality'. The United States was born on the Atlantic seaboard of the political wisdom of colonial leaders; the American nation was born in the Mississippi Valley of the practical needs of the incoming people. Each was to fit itself to the other.

But America did not acquire a distinctive national spirit until the first generation had passed from the stage. 'Until about the year 1820', writes Professor Hadley, '...the United States remained in many essential features a group of English colonies, separated from the mother country in 1776, somewhat against their will, by the want of tact of George III and his ministers, and united with one another in 1788, also somewhat against their will, by the extraordinary tact of the leaders of the Constitutional Convention'.[1] In the years immediately following the War of 1812–14 we discern the birth of a national spirit, democratic and American, spreading from the West to the Atlantic Coast. This new conception becomes the governing force in American history. Having made a state, to make a nation. State rights and sectional differences, geographical separation and racial diversity yield to the idea of an American nation. The relations of peoples within the United States

[1] Hadley, A. T., *Undercurrents in American Politics*, p. 14.

have been governed by this ideal of national unity.

Farseeing statesmen also envisaged the future for which the Westerners were laying the foundation. At a time when New England was showing a strongly separatist feeling (1809), one of her leading men, John Quincy Adams, was pleading with William Plumer for history written from a national point of view, not New England histories or Virginian histories. 'Historical works, honestly and judiciously executed', he writes, will best counteract the tendency of the states to 'partial and foolish combinations'. The doctrine of union is 'the fundamental maxim to be confirmed'. Let New England exhibit the brightest example of 'a truly liberal and comprehensive American system'.[1] Publius, in *The Federalist*, had earlier struck the note of 'one great American system, superior to the control of all transatlantic force or influence, and able to dictate the terms of the connection between the old and the new world'.[2]

At the same time, from the bench of the Supreme Court, Chief Justice Marshall was enlarging the scope of the National Government and establishing its authority. 'America', he said, in a famous

[1] *Writings of John Quincy Adams*, III, p. 341.
[2] *The Federalist*, edited by Lodge, H. C., p. 67.

decision in 1821, 'has chosen to be, in many respects, and to many purposes, a nation',[1] and he was determined to make her government equal to that choice. The claims of the states were kept within due bounds and political unity increased.

In the stirring years of the Revolution there were vigorous advocates of a national language and system of education and culture to inspire patriotism, confidence and a bond of union. But distinctive culture is the offspring of time, and it was not by that agency, but in its advocacy of freedom and equality, that the new republic was to find a unifying idea, an image of itself and a sense of its uniqueness and mission in the world. Jefferson gave confident expression to this ideal now born in the American people. 'He believed the young nation had been singled out by Providence to become the embodiment of the national and liberal ideals of the eighteenth century.'[2] Here was something to capture the spirit of men— to infuse a common faith and purpose in a growing multitude who lacked the ties of blood and history and religion and the integration of an older social order. As 'the sole depository of the sacred fire of

[1] *Heritage of America*, p. 228.
[2] Kohn, H., *The Idea of Nationalism*, p. 308.

freedom and self government', America would become a place of refuge for the oppressed of all nations and an example to the states of the Old World. 'I like the dreams of the future', he wrote, 'better than the history of the past.'[1]

An American government, an American man, an American nation, an American ideal—so was shaped the mould into which the diverse races of Europe were received.

Down to 1810 the remarkable growth of population was for the most part natural. Immigration was not the prime cause. But from 1820 the number of foreigners entering the United States mounted rapidly. In the 'thirties half a million came from Europe, in the 'forties a million and a half, and in the 'fifties two and a half million. They came from the same countries as in colonial days, chiefly from Great Britain, Ireland and Germany. To the Americans there seemed unlimited space. Jefferson had spoken of 'a chosen country with room enough for our descendants to the thousandth and thousandth generation'.[2]

Those who prospered sent money and exhortation to their friends to follow. 'This is the country for a man to enjoy himself', writes an Englishman to his

[1] Kohn, *op. cit.*, p. 276.
[2] Inaugural Address, 1801, *Heritage of America*, p. 217.

brother in 1818, 'prairie...at two dollars an acre...
tea, coffee, beef, fowls, pies, eggs, pickles, good
bread; and their favourite beverage is whisky or
peach brandy. Say is it so in England?'[1]

The stream was flowing. But, to the outside
observer, neither its immediate effects, nor its
future possibilities, were apparent. Carlyle, writing
to Emerson in 1839, foresees, as Adam Smith had
done, the future growth of America, but he sees it
as Anglo-Saxon, 'the ties of the two parishes,
Mother and Daughter, getting closer and closer
knit. Indissoluble ties. I reckon (he goes on) that
this huge smoky Wen may, for some centuries yet,
be...a yearly meeting place for "All the Saxons".
...After centuries, if Boston, if New York, have
become the most convenient "All Saxondom" we
will right cheerfully go thither to hold such
festival.'[2] But this was not to be the destiny of
New York or Boston. Nor was Emerson more
gifted with prophetic vision, for he saw in the
American only the continuation of the English
character in new conditions.

Meanwhile Irish and German emigrants were
increasing in numbers. The Irish came in a stream
with the famine caused by the failure of the potato

[1] *Heritage of America*, p. 262. Cf. Dickens, *American Notes* (Everyman), p. 221.
[2] Gordon, G. S., *Anglo-American Literary Relations*, p. 55.

(23)

crop in 1845 and 1846. For the next few years they averaged 200,000 a year. Before the end of the century Ireland had sent four million of her people to the United States. The Irish went to New England and the North Atlantic and North Central States, and especially into the towns and construction camps. A great programme of roads, canals and public works was going forward and their labour was welcome.

The Germans included at first a good many political refugees and intellectuals, but after 1850 economic causes stimulated an exodus of peasants, mechanics and labourers. They distributed themselves more evenly in the country than other immigrants, but in general favoured the Western States, and Wisconsin at one time seemed likely to become a German state. Law-abiding, industrious and intelligent, they were generally welcome, though their social customs caused some friction with settlers of Puritan descent, upholders of temperance and Sabbath observance. On the whole their American record is good, though one scans it in vain for evidence of a master race.

The rise of the great political parties facilitated the assimilation of the immigrants. Party politics gives value to the citizen; the voter has a friend. The Democrats, in particular, laid hold of them, for Whigs and Republicans were suspected of anti-foreign prejudice. To capture the immigrant vote, the Democratic party had from 1840 to 1856 a special plank in its platform:

'That the liberal principles...which make ours the land of liberty, and the asylum of the oppressed of every nation, have ever been cardinal principles in the democratic faith; and every attempt to abridge the present privilege of becoming citizens, and the owners of soil amongst us, ought to be resisted....'[1]

Some apprehensions were aroused. The Irish and Germans were mainly Catholics, and Catholics wanted their own schools. But Americans already saw in the common school the great nationalising agency. The common school, said the *Minnesota Chronicle* in 1850, places the child of the immigrant on the same bench with the native. As he plays with his schoolfellow he learns to sing 'Hail Columbia', and before he leaves the desk for the plough, he is as sturdy a little republican as may be found in the land.[2]

Others complained of the flocking of emigrants to the populous towns of the Middle West. Intemperate, unused to the comforts of life and

[1] Porter, K. H., *National Party Platforms*, pp. 3, etc.
[2] Stephenson, G. M., *A History of American Immigration*, p. 101.

(25)

regardless of its proprieties, they were creating a new social problem.

The political influence of the immigrant and the vague disquiet caused by their increasing numbers awoke at last an organised opposition. In 1854 was formed the Supreme Order of the Star-Spangled Banner, popularly known as the Know-Nothing Party. Their principle was that Americans must rule America. They demanded that native-born citizens be selected for all state, federal and municipal offices and that the law of naturalisation be changed and twenty-one years' residence be required for citizenship.[1] The Party achieved nothing, for the issue they raised was swallowed up in the rising conflict concerning slavery.

In general Americans welcomed the foreigner. What they objected to was any attempt to perpetuate foreign languages and customs, any divisive influences in their life. It was from the West that the warmest welcome came. There, was the greatest need for labour; there, society was most free from convention and assimilation easiest. So the immigrant found his place, and the vote and the freehold consolidated him with the nation. Southerners did not favour immigration. They saw

[1] *Documents of American History*, edited by Commager, H. S., I, 337 (2nd ed.).

that the immigrants went chiefly to the northern and western states and strengthened the North. New England also retained her old character. Foreign labourers began to flow into her towns; but the native population kept itself separate, and the daughters of the farmers withdrew from the factories, where the Irish replaced them. The competition of North and South for the western lands made immigrants still more welcome in the North, for Scandinavians and Germans were against the extension of slavery. Kansas, said one politician, must be made German, if necessary, in order that it may be made free. How strange the words sound to-day!

At the decisive electoral struggle of 1860 the vote of the immigrants was of critical importance. In some states they held the balance of power. The slavery issue caused a shift of allegiance. While the Irish stuck to the Democrats, Germans, Scandinavians and Dutch went over to the Republicans and helped them to win the North-West. Thereafter, the immigration plank disappears from the Democratic platform, and in 1864 it was the Republicans who maintained that foreign immigration had added to the wealth and power of the nation and should be fostered by a liberal and just policy.[1]

[1] Porter, *op. cit.* p. 62.

Westward the Americans traversed a relatively empty continent. Indians did not become citizens, and in time the tribes were placed on reservations. But there were descendants of French colonists in Louisiana, Spaniards in New Mexico and California, and a mixture of peoples in East Florida. In the Mississippi Valley old names speak for the original French settlements—St Louis, Vincennes, Terre Haute. The old Creole families of Louisiana desired to preserve their language and manner of life. But the energy of the incoming Americans overflowed them. In New Orleans, the faubourg Marigny was soon outclassed by the faubourg St Mary, and an enterprising American city displaced the sleepy bayou on its outskirts.

To Castile and Leon Columbus gave a new world. Such was the motto posthumously inscribed on the arms of Columbus. And still in Santa Fé the Spaniard makes his claim of precedence. He is the native American; later comers are Anglo-Americans, the 'Anglos'. The New Mexican legislature has always been bilingual. Santa Fé and Quebec are the only places in North America where the government is conducted in two languages. But schools are carried on in English, intermarriage is fusing the two races and New Mexico assimilates itself to the other states.

California had the same mixed society as the other Spanish colonies—a few Creole families of pure Spanish blood, and then, writes Richard Henry Dana in 1840, from this upper class they go down by regular shades...to the pure Indian. The Americans and English who reside here, he adds, become Catholics to a man, the current phrase among them being, 'A man must leave his conscience at Cape Horn'.[1] The inundation of gold-seekers and the annexation to the United States, following the Mexican War, speedily transformed California, but the old missions and place-names recall its Spanish origins.

Thus transcontinental expansion was accomplished without raising any serious problems of the relations of peoples. The rapid spread of American civilisation, fostered by all the modern arts, still leaves some islands of an older life, unsubmerged in the sea of modern uniformity, but no centres whence a different national tradition may spread.

All this while the Union nursed within its bosom the two views of the negro inherited from colonial days. Was he man, 'created equal', or chattel? The makers of the Union kept the word slavery out of the Constitution, but the fact remained. On this issue the course of events had given the country no

[1] *Heritage of America*, p. 517.

peace. As the Northern States emancipated their slaves the geographical frontier of the two views was defined, and the division between North and South appeared. The competition for the western lands sharpened the antagonism. Opinion crystallised in two philosophies of social relations. The South claimed to have formed a different society, a society composed of two races, in which equality was not the right of man, but of a few only. National unity was threatened. In 1855 Lincoln posed the inevitable question: 'Can we as a nation continue together *permanently—for ever*—half slave and half free?'[1] The Union must 'become all one thing or all the other'.

It was not simply the status of the negro that was at stake, but the whole theory of the social order, the democratic faith which was guiding the creation of the American nation. Slavery was defended by a political philosophy opposed to democracy, and democracy was the great power which was making one nation of a medley of peoples. The struggle to preserve the union was a struggle to preserve democracy, and the struggle to preserve democracy was a struggle for the being of the nation.

The result of the Civil War was that the principle

[1] *Speeches and Letters of Abraham Lincoln*, p. 35 (Everyman ed.).

of democracy survived. In the trying years of reconstruction an effort was made to apply it to the negro. The XIIIth amendment to the Constitution secured this freedom. Further amendments attempted to secure him political and civil rights. Never in the history of social change was so much expected so quickly. But carpet-bag government could not lay the foundations of a new order. The South resisted and would not endure the Northern reconstruction of its life. When Governor Chamberlain was defeated in South Carolina in 1876, the last carpet-bag government fell. To William Lloyd Garrison, that ardent champion of emancipation, he wrote that his defeat had been inevitable —'the uneducated negro was too weak, no matter what his numbers, to cope with the whites'.[1] The political wisdom enshrined in the Supreme Court, which has adapted the American Constitution to the circumstances of the nation, rescued the South from an intolerant and intolerable haste. Legislation to secure the negro civil and social rights was declared unconstitutional. The transition was slowed down. Means were found by the South to deprive the negro of political influence, and the principle of social and cultural segregation was adopted. The religious life of the negroes had

[1] *Commager Documents*, II, 96.

become separate by their voluntary action. Schools were made separate by law. Separate accommodation was provided in public conveyances and places. Thus, throughout a part of the country, the new relations of the races are organised on a basis of social separation.

Since the Civil War, a third of the negro population has moved to other parts where there is no legal discrimination in education and political life. Economic opportunities and public amenities are not generally as open to them as to other races, and race conflict is liable to break out where the poor white and the negro come into economic competition.

To raise the negro to the standard of American democracy, and give him equal part in its functioning, is clearly a process—a process which does not simplify itself into a single problem. Successive generations will have to find their own solution of the difficulties it presents at each stage. Racial questions of similar character exist in other countries and are not likely to disappear in our time.

The Civil War was followed by a greatly increased influx from Europe. The tide of immigration swelled again. Between 1860 and 1930, twenty-eight million people entered the United States from Europe. Congress opened the door wider to the immigrant and the Homestead Act of 1863 offered free grants of land. A great age of industrial expansion was beginning and employers welcomed the cheap labour which Europe could supply. In the United States the balance was shifting from agriculture to industry, from country to town. The opportunities of employment were immense and of all kinds. American industrial development tended to eliminate skill, and the unskilled labourers who formed so large a proportion of the immigrants could quickly learn a simple job. At the same time means of transport improved and multiplied, the great shipping lines were seeking passengers, and their agents spread about Europe stimulating emigration. Better facilities for remitting money made it easy for the prosperous immigrant to bring over relatives and friends. Shipping agents and remittances probably stimulated more emigration than any other causes.

Hitherto, almost all the emigrants had been from Northern and Western Europe, but as these parts of Europe became industrialised, and as their birth-rate fell, they provided a diminishing proportion. The turn of Southern and Eastern Europe had come, and quickly the stream from these parts grew. Half of the later immigration came from them. The new emigrants were Italians, Greeks,

Slavs from Austria-Hungary, Jews, Poles, Finns and Lithuanians from Russia. These peoples had not shown the initiative, or acquired the habit of emigration, until the inducements were brought to their door. But the idea, once sown, grew and flourished. In the twentieth century the new emigration was nearly three times the volume of the old, and Italy displaced Germany as the chief source. The Scandinavians alone of the North-Western nations were keeping up their numbers. The American fever still spread through their villages and the young men were drawn away to the big American farms.

Particular industries attracted particular races. Slav emigrants went mainly into the heavy industries and mining and packing. Italians, Poles and Slovenes displaced the British or native American worker in the Pennsylvania mines, and, in the New England cotton mills, Greeks, Poles, Russians and Italians were employed instead of French Canadians and Irish. Jews and Italians took possession of the New York clothing trade, which had been American, English and Scotch; and Russians and Poles substituted themselves for Germans, English and Irish in the paper industry. It was the competition of lower standards of living.

With the change in the labour employed in

industry, the population of different quarters of cities changed its character. New York, which Carlyle had envisaged as a centre of Anglo-Saxondom, had become an international city. If coloured by nationalities, writes Jacob Riis in 1890, 'it would show more stripes than the zebra and more colours than any rainbow'. Ethnic cohesion is a natural consequence of large-scale immigration. In 1843 Lord Morpeth, travelling in the United States, remarked the existence of a colony of Yorkshiremen near Jacksonville on the prairie. Such segregation was even more natural to foreign races, and the urban and industrial expansion of the country immensely promoted it. The earlier immigrants had spread themselves evenly between land and industry. But free farms were gone by the twentieth century and most of the employment was in the towns. Hence the growing concentration of Irish, Italians, Slavs, Greeks and other races in the large cities, where, by 1930, 80% of the foreign-born were to be found.

The new stream greatly diversified the racial composition of the American people, and the process of assimilation presented new problems. Assimilation depends on willingness on both sides, and on the numbers on both sides. The majority of the immigrants still came with the intention of becoming American. But their geographical and economic distribution affected their opportunities. The habits and outlook of individuals can be changed when they have no root in the life of a group which offers opposition to assimilation. But foreigners gathered in large cities tended to keep their own language, have their own newspapers and social clubs, churches and schools, and to live as a separate community, and they were easily manipulated by the politicians. Many were ignorant and illiterate, liable to be victimised, and confronted with an increasing race prejudice.

Jacob Riis, a Danish immigrant, in his *Making of an American*, shows the difficulties attending the newcomer, and reveals, too, the attractive power of American citizenship. He tells us how, on his return to Denmark, he lay sick and despondent at Elsinore, when, suddenly, from his window he saw in the harbour below the Stars and Stripes floating in the breeze, and springing up on his bed to wave his hands, he knew that he had become an American in truth.[1]

While the immigrants contributed immensely to the rapid growth of the country and exhibited to the world America's great tradition of hospitality, their growing numbers and changing race distri-

[1] P. 443.

bution had begun to awaken questionings before the nineteenth century ended. What would be the effect of unrestricted immigration on the unity and character of the American nation? America wished to be rich, and wished to be hospitable, but she wished also to remain essentially what she was—to preserve the character of her political and social life. Had all the immigrants the capacity for democratic government—the intelligence, the man-liness, the power of co-operation it required? How long would it take the schools, the newspapers, the common language, the practice of political life, all the totality of American influences, to bring them up to the democratic level? Organised labour was becoming hostile. While the employer welcomed a stream of low-priced labour to keep down produc-tion costs, the employee would limit the supply to raise wages. Protestant sentiment became anxious about the Catholic influx from Southern and Eastern Europe, which for thirty years, 1877–1907, provided half the immigrants. The Pacific Coast was opposed to Oriental immigration. In that matter, a precedent had already been set. Chinese immigration was prohibited in 1882, and Japanese restricted by a gentleman's agreement in 1907. But the country was demanding further action. Political parties began to change their planks. All sensed the growing feeling and asked for restriction.

From 1897 Congress attempted to impose a literacy test, but successive Presidents vetoed the Bill. Woodrow Wilson declared it (1915) 'a radical departure from the traditional and long established policy of this country and from the very mission and spirit of the nation in respect of its relations to the peoples of the world'.[1] Illiteracy might denote, not incapacity, but lack of opportunity. Jefferson had used similar language; but in 1917 the Bill was passed over the President's veto.

The Great War disclosed a new aspect of the question. Hitherto external events had not excited racial sentiment in a manner to create internal dissension. But the rise of the German Empire produced unexpected reactions. There was a stirring in the graveyard of Europe. German feeling was strongly aroused. Social clubs were no longer so innocent of political object. President Wilson spoke out against the hyphenated Americans who set the land of their birth before the land of their adoption. A possible danger was revealed. Was America providentially destined to escape the race problems of Europe? Might not the sleeping racial sentiments be wakened to internal strife?

[1] Stephenson, *op. cit.*, pp. 166–7.

Following the War, came apprehensions of a mighty flood of immigrants from the Old World, distracted and bankrupt. There was dread of increasing unemployment, of an influx of revolutionary opinion, which would add to the social unrest. America began to doubt whether her future could be left to the play of natural forces. The country, it was argued, had reached the point of saturation and could no longer fully assimilate the foreign elements. So opinion shifted, and, as often happens in America, when it moves, it moves quickly. Within a few years the policy of restriction was accepted by the great majority of Americans as a social and political necessity.

The legislation of the 'twenties restricted the number of immigrants to a maximum of 150,000 a year, divided amongst the various nationalities on a quota system fixed according to the national origins of the American people. Persons not eligible for citizenship were excluded, and only white persons and persons of African descent are eligible. America looked back to 1790—the starting-point of an American people; the earlier stocks had blended well and to them the new policy gave a decided preference. So the door was closed. Within was a nation of 120 million people, an offshoot of Northern Europe, and determined to keep that character.

Long ago Disraeli bade us turn our eyes to the young nations growing up beyond the seas. But our historians and our people have followed with more attention the rise of nationalism on the European than on the American continent. Yet the making of the American nation is the most important development of modern times. It will fill a greater page of future history than the unification of Italy or Germany.

Three-fifths of the population to-day is of British and Irish origin; there is great diversity of race in the remainder. When we talk to a soldier lad in the street we do well to remember that, while he may be descended from a Pilgrim Father or a hero of Bunker Hill, it is more likely that he is the son of a Bavarian peasant or a Scandinavian farmer or an Italian shopkeeper or a Greek shepherd or a Bohemian or Polish mechanic, and we may well wonder at the assimilative power of American civilisation which has given him a new language and inspired him with a faith in national and individual freedom.

How has so much been achieved? We look on at one of the greatest social and political experiments of history—an experiment in the welding of mankind. We see it in its process—already on an unequalled scale an unequalled achievement. We see

the present problems. The result—the future
American nation—we shall not see. But in outline
the process of its growth is clear. If we turn our
eyes for a moment from the conditions of to-day—
the problems of assimilation, all the bubbling of the
melting-pot and its unmelted lumps, to the mould
into which its content has been and is being
poured, we see the races being made into a nation
by conditions, material and ideal, which create a
common life, common ideas and a community of
purpose.

The authority of the national government over-
rode the divisive tradition of state rights. The
triumphant achievements of the great railways gave
the continent physical unity and overcame the
natural effects of geographical sectionalism. The
directing ideas in economic development came
largely from New England and the North Atlantic
states. From this centre went forth the men whose
organising ability marshalled the labour of Europe
in the colonisation of the West. A single type of
life, spreading from a single centre, with the facility
with which men and goods and ideas move in
America, created the economic unity of the country.
Modern invention speeded the process. Free trade
over the whole area assimilated the mechanism of
daily existence, the habits of the people, their food

and dress. Wherever the immigrant went he entered into the same kind of life and was caught up into its activities.

This was the material frame of unity; not less important is the spirit. The intense concentration on material things has not submerged the ideal side of American life. 'Land of unprecedented faith', wrote Whitman. The ideals of the founders of the republic—the faith in liberty and equality, the belief in man and the belief in progress—have not been lost. The vastness and bounty of nature, pride in the national history, the prevailing energy, the sense of great achievement and of confidence in the future—these create the atmosphere in which the great task of making a nation of such diverse elements has been essayed. All through its history the country has been animated by the sense of a mission. Crudely or spiritually expressed, it is always present. 'A spirit of brotherhood', writes a recent American historian, 'transcending class, race, and religion, a feeling that all dwellers within these states are partners in a common enterprise, is the peculiar quality that brought the American Republic into being.'[1] That unique power of inspiring men of diverse races with a common faith is the greatest force of assimilation.

[1] Commager, H. S., *The Growth of the American Republic*, II, 591–2.

To an assemblage of people, without the ties of race, religion and history, of common inheritance and background, the democratic faith is the essential bond. It is this which creates the magic of American citizenship and makes America an idea as well as a place.

And here a word must be said of education—'the best safeguard of democracy', as President Eliot of Harvard described it—and of religion, so powerful to unite or divide. From the beginning, educational opportunity and religious liberty have been of vital importance in the making of the nation. No country has been more conscious of the importance of education or more abundant in its educational enterprise. Social integration and the use of a common language are essential to democracy. To the common school the country looks to draw the immigrant out of his race group and to spread common ideas and social habits and the sense of pride in belonging to the American nation. The ignorance and illiteracy of so many immigrants makes the burden heavy and the process slow.

The national government placed religion outside of politics: 'Congress shall make no law respecting an establishment of religion or prohibiting the free exercise thereof.' So runs the first amendment to the Constitution. In a land without religious establishments and historic feuds and jealousies, the divisive force of religion is reduced to a minimum, and an impediment to assimilation and unity is removed. There has been no unifying influence of a national Church. Yet it may be that Christianity has more influence to unite the population under conditions of complete freedom, where all forms of religion abound, than it has where one form is established by law. 'Religious freedom', it has been said, 'is more than a private right, it is an American necessity.'

What has been true of religion has been true of other divisive forces in European history. Wendell Willkie summed up the matter thus in his book, *One World*:

> We have created a strong nation because these new arrivals did not have the distractions, under our form of government, of continually opposing and battling one another, but entered as partners into the general upbuilding and consolidation.... The height of our civilisation has been reached... by the ability of peoples of varying beliefs and of different racial extractions to live side by side in the United States with common understanding, respect and helpfulness.[1]

What is the significance of the racial factor in American history? South African history is domin-

[1] See pp. 157–9.

ated by it, Canadian much influenced. But in the United States there has been no race sectionalism— no concentration of one people in a particular area, like the French Canadians in Quebec. None of the American states has a national basis; all were artificially formed, so far as their race character is concerned. And the larger groupings in the country, the sections, have a unity of economic, not racial, interest.

Nor in the great movements of American history have the race differences asserted themselves. Perhaps here there has been safety in numbers; for, while two races will contend for the mastery, many will more easily unite their efforts in a common task. Taken as a whole, the vast immigration contributed substantially to the settlement of the West, to industrial expansion and to political unity. The uniformity of American civilisation to-day impresses the traveller more than the diversity of the peoples.

While the great names in American history have a familiar sound to us, we observe the contribution of the foreign strains to American culture in recent times—to literature, the fine arts and music, to religion, science and learning. Many of America's leading writers to-day do not bear Anglo-Saxon names.[1] Are they, as has been said, 'a foreign

[1] Gordon, *op. cit.* p. 110.

(45)

patch on the American quilt', or are they truly national? Whence is their inspiration? Such a question looks beyond our sight. Only the future can reveal the influence of the different peoples in the formation of national character and culture.

It must be admitted that the ideal of American democracy and American unity has not been seriously challenged from without. Few external events have tended to precipitate racial feeling, for most immigrants have been glad to leave the Old World behind them. The Irish, indeed, are slow to forget or forgive the wrongs of their race and have generally exerted their influence in an anti-English sense. 'It must always be borne in mind', wrote Sir Lionel Sackville-West from Washington to Lord Granville in 1884, 'that the object of the Irish party here is to create ill-feeling between the two countries',[1] and members of Congress dependent on the Irish vote will use language much stronger than their real sentiments. A feeling of this kind might be a cause of trouble in international relations, but not a peril to national unity. Even if Hitler in 1940 had triumphed in Europe and Africa, if South America had fallen to the Axis, and he had made an appeal to racial sentiment in the United

[1] *Private Letters from the British Embassy in Washington*, 1880–5, edited by Knaplund, P. and Clewer, C. M., p. 178.

States, it is unlikely that he could have endangered internal unity. Nazi philosophy was never acceptable to American democracy.

In America, then, we conclude that the differences of the European peoples have had no major political significance. The manner of settlement and the assimilative power of American civilisation reduced them from major to minor influences. Foreign elements are not grouped in the states in such numbers as to capture the machinery of government, though this may happen in towns. Appeals to race feeling have been of local and temporary significance, and not concerning great issues of national policy. The unifying influence of political life varies with local circumstances, but steadily prevails.

Willkie alludes in his book to the 'maladjustments of the races'. He sees much remaining to be done if America is to realise her ideals. This is doubtless true. But the historian who is dealing not with the problems of contemporary politics, but reviewing the whole story, may justly conclude that the American experiment has achieved an amazing success and that nowhere is anything equal to it seen. The process is unfinished; the mutual assimilation of the races continues; assimilation is not amalgamation, and we know too little about the

(47)

usion of races to visualise the America of the future. But the hopes of the founders were not extravagant. The settlement of America was, to use the words of John Adams in 1765, 'the opening of a grand scene'.[1] 'A nation', said Disraeli, 'is a work of art and a work of time.' Certainly, they who build a nation out of earth's many races must have an ideal for their ally and take patience into their politics. This the size of the country and the variety of its people emphasise for the United States. But the extent to which unification has already proceeded, and the firm faith and intention that it shall proceed, seem likely to make true the national motto, *e pluribus unum.*

[1] Quoted in Kohn, *op. cit.* p. 273.